bless
my
child

A Catholic Mother's Prayer Book

bless
my
child

Julie Cragon

ave maria press AmP Notre Dame, Indiana

© 2005 by Ave Maria Press, Inc.

www.avemariapress.com

International Standard Book Number: 1-59471-014-7

Cover painting by Rose Walton

Cover and text design by Katherine Robinson Coleman

Printed and bound in the United States of America.

Library of Congress Cataloging-in-Publication Data

Library of Congress Cataloging-in-Publication Data

Cragon, Julie, 1960-
  Bless my child : a Catholic mother's prayer book / Julie Cragon.
      p. cm.
  ISBN 1-59471-014-7 (pbk.)
  1. Mothers—Prayer-books and devotions—English. 2. Catholic Church—Prayer-books and devotions—English. I. Title.

  BV4847.C73 2005
  242'.8431—dc22

                                                    2004026346

Contents

Introduction

As I sit amidst the hundreds of parents at a meeting before the start of school, the principal proceeds to inform us that the school will not have as many fundraisers this year. As a substitute for the time families spent on fundraising projects, she challenges us to bring our children to a family holy hour each month. She says, "When it comes to what's really important," referring to praying for our children, "If not us, who? If not here, where? If not now, when?"

I admit, I rarely listen at these meetings. With six children passing through the same routine every year, I feel like I've heard it all. But this truly touched me spiritually. I began immediately praying specifically for my children. Not praying that I will be a good mother to them or that I will keep them safe and warm, but that my children will be nourished and fed and led by the light of Christ, his mother, the saints, and the holy men and women given to us as examples.

My prayer is that mothers will use this prayer book, these words I've been given from the Spirit, to pray our children through life. Our children are our future, the future of the Church, as we hear countless times from Pope John Paul II. And who better than our children to turn this world to Christ? Who better to hear and to see and to feel the love of Christ so deeply that they want to pass that on to others, to "go out to all the world"?

How to Use This Book

As mothers, we instinctively know that we need to pray for our children. We also face many demands on our time and often feel there is no time to pray. As a mother of six, I feel that way more often that I care to admit. But I've also found that it is easier than we might think, and that it is one of the most loving and important things that we can do for our children. I hope this book will help you throughout your day, and be your prayer companion throughout the life of your child.

This book features prayers that we can use throughout their lives and at different stages of life (as a toddler, middle school child, teenager, adult). I've also included a section of prayers for difficult, serious circumstances, which unfortunately seem to touch the life of every mother and child. The prayer titles name specific circumstances and needs. The table of contents helps you find them this way.

The easiest times to pray are when the children are sleeping at early morning, naptime, or after they're in bed. Older children offer additional times—after they've left for school, or better yet, with them before they leave for school. This builds their prayer life and increases their sense of security. When they hear you pray for them, your children hear and feel your love and the love of God.

Of course, there are some days that really seem to offer you no breaks. A teething baby may need your comfort for twenty-four hours. A trip to the emergency room can seem endless. You may feel able to only pray "God, please help us, strengthen us, comfort us. Bless my child." Go ahead. This prayer is good and can repeated as often as needed.

Whether you keep this book on your night stand, in your purse, in the kitchen, in your desk at work, or somewhere else, I hope it helps you join me in praying our children through life. May God bless our children.

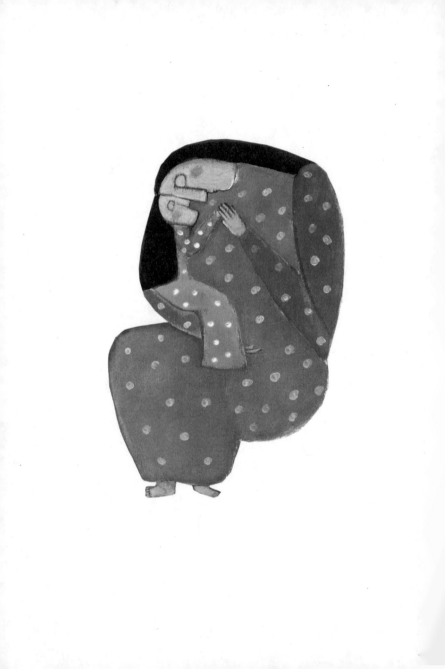

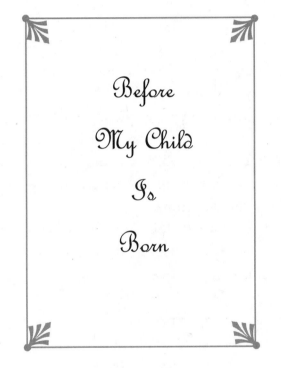

Before

My Child

Is

Born

Unborn Child

St. Gerard, patron of expectant mothers,
Pray for this unborn child
  that he may be healthy upon his birth
  and throughout his life.
As my child grows, may he feel my love for him more
  each day
  and may his tiny body be nourished properly.
Obtain for us the grace to stay close to God
  and to follow His will as you did.
St. Gerard, mothers are often asked to do two or more
  tasks at the same time.
Ask God to bless this child with a patient mother
  who gives of herself more than she feels
  she actually has to give;
  a mother filled with the wisdom
  and the courage to persevere.
May this unborn child be raised in strong faith and
  conviction so that he may someday
  spend eternal life in heaven.
Amen.

Giving Birth

O Most Blessed Young Mother of the Child Jesus,
    you know the physical pains of birth,
shift our focus from the gifts God has in store for us.
Pray for me that this gift, this child, may remain in my
    heart and in my mind,
    that my labor may be quick, and that,
    as I picture you, Holy Mother,
    alone with Joseph in the stable at Bethlehem,
    shivering with cold, giving birth to Jesus,
    may our joys be complete.
With each push to bring forth this miracle,
    help my child to feel your loving presence and
    strength.
Please intercede that our gift from God may be healthy
    and flawless.
Show mercy upon our baby and ask God to grace us
    with a loving, Christ-centered home
    for all our child's life.
Amen.

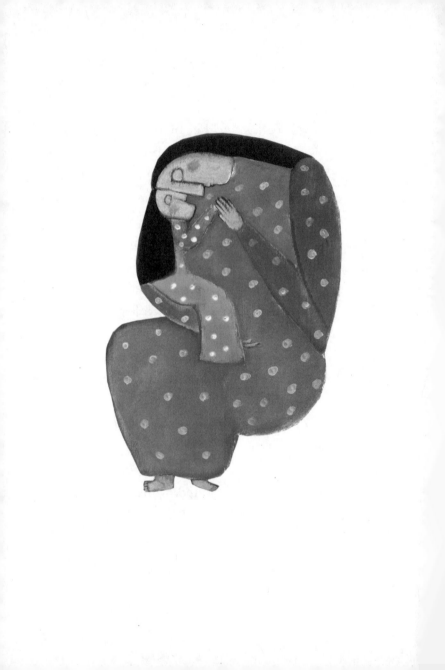

For

My Newborn

and

Infant

Child

In Celebration

Lord, thank You.
Thank You for this beautiful child
You have loaned me.
Thank You for the indescribable way
    she occupies my mind and my heart.
I am grateful for the joys and for the struggles we
    share.
I know they all go with the demands of parenthood.
Remind me to cherish every moment,
    for they will soon seem so few and far between.
This child of God is such a precious gift; teach me to
    appreciate her.
Lord, I know that this beautiful, wonderful creation
    is straight from Your heart;
    help me to share her delight with others and to
    handle her with care.
Amen.

Morning Offering

Lord, may this child be led to follow Your ways
   by hands full of strength.
May this child feel safe and secure in Your name
   in arms filled with warmth to hold him.
May this child be filled with Your love
   and a giving heart.
May this child's needs be seen
   and may he be taught by a mouth
   that speaks Your truth.
May this child be guided down Your path of
   righteousness by good example.
And, may this child be understood all his life
   by parents filled with the loving presence
   of Christ.
   Today and every day, he may be guided down the
   road that leads directly back to You.
Amen.

Adopted Child

Lord, my adopted child knows daily
  how special she is to this family.
Help her to quickly feel comfortable and loved.
Give her the gift of gentle transition.
She has filled a space in my life
  that I never realized was so great.
Help her to be filled with the faith of this family
  and to know Your love as we do.
Help her to turn to You in her needs.
Lord, hold her gently in Your loving care.
Amen.

Instructions

$\mathcal{L}$ord, each morning I start my day by praying for
Your guidance.

And yet, as the day goes by and my child tests me,

I wonder why he did not come with some sort of
instruction manual,

some kind of reference book that tells exactly how to
keep him on track,

to teach him Your ways.

Remind me, Lord, to turn to Your word daily,

to teach my child Your unconditional love.

to pass Your lessons on to my child.

May this child understand Your word and practice
what You preach.

I pray that I will sow and nourish good seed.

Lead this child to the events that give him the grace to
someday return to You.

Help this child take the small amounts I have to offer
and send Your Spirit to take care of the rest.

Amen.

Teething

St. Appollonia,

Pray that God might ease the pain in my child's mouth
as she's teething.

Her red, swollen gums are hurting her,
causing her to rub her face.

She doesn't understand this hurt.

She's fussy and confused.

Ask God to help me to have patience with her
fussiness;
and to help soothe her aches and pains.

Be with us in our days and nights, and aid us in our
perseverance.

Pray that this suffering helps us draw closer to God.

Amen.

First Words

Lord, my child said her first word today.
Oh what joy to witness another milestone in her life.
Just one word, and yet this is confirmation of her
    growth and her learning.
Help her to develop her language
    that she may praise You fully in voice.
May she use her words to speak Your truths and
    to teach and to preach Your message.
Yes Lord, today just one word, her first word,
    but the start of countless possibilities.
Guide her tongue as her speech develops.
Guard her as she grows.
Amen.

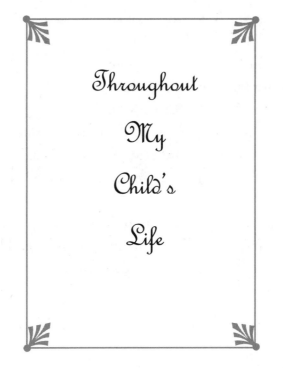

Throughout

My

Child's

Life

Prayers for the Sacraments

Baptism

Lord, may the waters of Baptism cleanse my child's
   soul.
May the oil of chrism be his salvation.
May he walk in the light of the Spirit and
   keep the flame of faith alive in his heart.
May his white garment of purity surround him and
   remain as an outward sign of Christian dignity.
We are thankful for the commitment his Godparents
   have made
   and ask You to aid them in their duties.
Lord, keep this child of Yours pure in mind and heart,
and bestow on everyone attending this baptism the
graces given
   by our own renewed baptismal promises.
Amen.

Reconciliation

Merciful Father, Lord of forgiveness, hear
    the requests of my child through Your priestly
    intercessor.
As he confesses what he believes and what the Church
    teaches is an offense against You,
    heal him of his wrongfulness.
Cleanse him body and soul, and bring him
    closer to You.
May his frequent confession gain him Your
    heavenly reward.
Amen.

First Communion

Dear Holy St. Tarcisius, be with my child
as he receives communion for the first time.
Teach him to love Jesus in the Eucharist as you did.
Help him to believe that his body is a tabernacle for
the Holy Eucharist.
Help my child to carry Christ to all those he meets.
Strengthen his faith and teach him to ask for a
greater love of Jesus each time he receives Holy
Communion.
Dear St. Tarcisius, be here with all of these children on
this special day.
Pray for them that they may always hold fast to their
beliefs and that
the Eucharist may give them the grace they need
to someday join in Christ's banquet in heaven.
Amen.

Note: St. Tarcisius died carrying the Blessed Sacrament
to those in prison.

Prayer Before Communion

Jesus, as I come to receive You
   in Your most Holy Sacrament,
   make me a worthy servant.
Allow me to offer up my communion for my child.
May she always know Your presence.
Amen.

Prayer After Communion

Jesus, I offer my communion as a blessing for my
child.
Bless his lips and his tongue that he may speak gently,
his hands that he may be led to You,
his head that he may know Your truths,
his eyes that he may see You clearly,
his ears that he may hear Your word and take it to
the world,
his feet that he may walk the path that leads to
You.
Amen.

Confirmation

Come Holy Spirit,
  fill my child with Your gifts of
  wisdom, understanding, counsel,
  fortitude, knowledge, piety, and fear of the Lord.
Increase her baptismal graces and strengthen her faith
  that she may become a true witness of Christ's
  teachings.
As she completes her mission begun at baptism and
  receives greater responsibility in her service to
  God,
  give her the strength she needs to defend her faith.
Show her the way to true discipleship.
Bless her sponsor that she may remain with her on this
  journey.
Enlighten this sponsor and give her the graces
  to lead my child in wisdom to
  spread Your name in word and deed.
Amen.

Altar Server

St. John Berchmans, guide my child as he assists at
Mass.

May he be an example of respect and reverence to the
most Blessed Sacrament.

Ask God to give him the graces
to serve all of mankind in God's name and
to love the sacrifice of the Mass with a pure heart.

May his service at Christ's holy altar bring him closer
to his eternal reward.

Amen.

Note: St. John Berchmans is patron of altar servers.

Marriage

Lord, bless these young people on their wedding day
and give them the wisdom to fully understand this
sacrament.

May the joy of this day last forever and
may they be blessed with children in the years
ahead.

May their love for one another
strengthen their relationship with You
so together they can work for the greater glory of
Your kingdom.

Amen

Characteristics and Virtues

Persistence

"And I tell you, ask and you will receive; seek and you will find; knock and the door will be opened to you. For everyone who asks, receives; and the one who seeks, finds; and to the one who knocks, the door will be opened."

Luke 11:9–10

Lord, teach my child to be persistent in her prayers.
Show her the way to You

through continued asking for her needs
and seeking Your voice.

She knows You are there; help her to remain constant
in her journey.
Help her to turn to you as to a trusted friend.
In her persistence, may she someday reach the door
that leads to your right hand.
Amen.

Responsibility

"*If* you choose you can keep the commandments;
it is loyalty to do His will."

Sirach 15:15

Lord, help my child to make responsible choices.
Teach her to pray to Your Holy Spirit in difficult and
uncertain times.
Show her the way to follow Your commandments
and to always take responsibility
for the choices she makes.
Hold her in the palm of Your hand.
Amen.

Trust

"My soul, be at rest in God alone, from whom comes my hope. God alone is my rock and my salvation, my secure height; I shall not fall. My safety and glory are with God, my strong rock and refuge. Trust God at all times, my people! Pour out your hearts to God our refuge."

Psalm 62:6–9

Lord, all things in this world are passing.
Who we can trust and what we can rely on are
    as temporary in this life as ice on hot pavement.
Teach my child to put all her trust in You.
Your promises are always solid;
    they will never melt away.
Help her in all times, good and bad;
    let her know You are her refuge.
Lord, teach my child to offer to You her soul
    and to know that with you she always has a place
    to pour out her heart.
Amen.

Wisdom

"For Wisdom is better than corals, and no choice possession can compare with her."

Proverbs 8:11

Lord, teach my child Your wisdom.
Show her Your ways and help her to pursue Your gift
    of wisdom
    that reveals to us the proper way to live.
Give her the gifts of understanding, righteousness,
    truth, knowledge, discretion, insight and strength.
Teach her all that is acceptable so she may diligently
    seek heaven.
Amen.

Faithfulness

Lady of Fatima,
>   as you appeared to Francisco, Jacinta, and Lucia,
>   stay ever present in the heart of my child.

Teach her to live a faithful life and to always ask
>   forgiveness for her sins.

Keep her close to you, most Blessed Mother.

Remind her to pray daily for the conversion of souls
>   and for peace in our world.

Oh most lovely Mother, through these children you
>   sent your message.

Help my child also be an instrument of your message
>   by her example throughout her life.

Amen.

Obedience

Lady of Guadalupe, as Juan Diego was so obedient
and persistent in your name,
make my child persistent and obedient in the Lord.
Mother of the Americas, help my child
to build a shrine in her heart in your honor
so that you will give her your love,
compassion, help, and protection
as you gave them to Juan Diego.
Merciful Mother, help my child to seek you and have
confidence in you.
You chose Juan Diego, one of the least,
to carry your message to the world.
Help my child to carry and to live your message.
Give her perseverance in her faith
and help her to obey your requests.
Amen.

Peace

"Then the wolf shall be a guest of the lamb, and the leopard shall lie down with the kid; the calf and the young lion shall browse together, with a little child to guide them."

Isaiah 11:6

Lord, show my child the road to peace
  at school, at home, between friends, in life.
Help her to have peace of mind and peace of heart.
Teach her to be an example of true peace in all she
  does
  so that someday, all who know her may share in the
  peaceable kingdom.
Amen.

Mercy

St. Faustina, pray that Christ might teach my child
His Divine Mercy.

Let her eyes be merciful that she may see the beauty in
others and
not judge by appearance.

Let her ears be merciful that she may hear the needs of
others.

Let her tongue be merciful that she may comfort
others and not talk about them.

Let her hands be merciful that she may do good deeds
for others.

Let her feet be merciful that she may help others and
never grow weary of serving them.

Let her heart be merciful that she may feel the
sufferings of others and comfort them,
no matter how much ridicule she may receive.

St. Faustina, pray that the Lord's mercy rest upon my
child.

Amen.

Purity

St. Maria Goretti, watch over my daughter.
Help her to stay pure in body, mind, and heart.
Keep her safe from all harm.
You gave your life to avoid sin;
    hourly, guide my daughter in her choices and
    free her from earthly temptations.
As you forgave your attacker, teach my child to forgive
    even those who hurt her the worst.
Give her peace—peace of mind and peace of heart.
Lead her in your way of purity.
Amen.

Strong Convictions

St. Dominic Savio, help my son
   to make
   God-centered decisions.
Teach him to have strong convictions
   toward reconciliation and communion as you did.
Keep him pure of mind, of body, and of heart.
Give him the wisdom to stay close to Christ.
Teach him the saving power of God's love and
   the promises for those who keep His commands.
May he walk in the light of Christ, following your
   example,
   and someday gain heaven.
Amen.

Note: St. Dominic Savio at a young age dedicated himself to God. He is regarded by the Church as an example of purity and piety.

Faith and Action

Blessed Brother Andre, through the intercession
of St. Joseph, you healed many people who
came to you.
Your incredible trust and belief in the power of
St. Joseph is a great example of faith.
Teach my child the saving power of the saints.
Help her to put faith in those powerful men and
women who have gone before us.
I'm not asking for her to be able to heal through
intercession as you did. Intercede for the simple
requests that can make her happy in this journey.
The more she knows about the lives of these great men
and women, the more she can request their help,
so that she may someday join them in the joy
of heaven.
Blessed Brother Andre, lead my child in faith and
action.
Amen.

Happiness

"He said to his disciples, 'Therefore I tell you, do not worry about your life and what you will eat, or about your body and what you will wear. For life is more than food and the body more than clothing. For where your treasure is, there also will your heart be.'"

Luke 12:22–23, 34

Lord, teach my child true happiness.
Show her the way to cast aside all her anxieties,
    to place all her cares into your hands.
Allow her to see the simple joys in life,
    the good things that happen every day.
Teach her that it is truly your good pleasure
    to give her everything she needs,
    to give her the happiness she deserves.
Amen.

46

Humility

"Do nothing out of selfishness or vainglory; rather, humbly regard others as more important than yourselves, each looking out not for his own interests, but [also] everyone for those of others."

Philippians 2:3–4

Lord, I pray for humility for my child.
Teach him to put on the mind of Christ and
    to humbly serve others.
Help him to understand that by
    caring for the interests of others,
    by putting others first, he is serving God.
Teach him to give without being noticed and
    without the need for something in return,
    as your truly humble servant.
Amen.

Judging Others

"Stop judging, that you may not be judged. For as you judge, so will you be judged, and the measure with which you measure will be measured out to you."

Matthew 7:1–2

Lord, this is one of the most difficult lessons for my child and
 I, too, have difficulty in not judging others.
Make me an example to my child,
 to teach her that how we treat others is how we will be treated, and fairly so.
We have no idea what others may be going through in their lives.
Help my child not to cast stones.
Teach her to worry about her own faults and
 not to judge, but to pray for others.
Amen.

Evil

St. Michael, defend my child against evil.
He's doing things that will harm him.
He's risking the loss of his friends, his school, and
    possibly his life.
I'm lost. I'm powerless against this hell here on earth.
Pierce his demons with your sword and shield him in
    God's mercy.
Shower him with the love of Christ
    and bring my boy back home.
Amen.

Devotion to the Sacred Heart of Jesus

St. Margaret Mary,

Pray for my child that he may long for devotion like
yours.

[Help him to be an example of the practice of first
Friday reception of Communion.]

May the picture of the Sacred Heart in our home
inspire him

and may his devotion to Christ grow daily.

Show us the way to His Most Sacred Heart

so we may obtain the graces necessary for
salvation.

Amen.

Pray the Rosary

St. Dominic, help me, as a mother,
    pass on to my children the practice of praying the
    rosary.
Show me, as Mary showed you, how to teach my
    children true devotion,
    so they may, through prayer, grow closer to God.
There could be no greater aid to heaven; no simpler
    request.
Teach me to show my children this way to salvation.
Amen.

Nine Day Novena

A novena is typically a series of prayers said for nine consecutive days invoking the intercession of a saint or Mary, or made directly to God. This novena may be said as it is written, or if one specific saint meets your child's need, use that same prayer for each of the nine days.

Specific examples of intentions addressed to particular saints:

St. Monica—that a child fallen away from the Church or questioning his faith may return to the Church

St. Anne—for a child not yet born, may grow up as a good child

Mary—that God's will for a child may be done

St. Maria Goretti—that a child may choose chastity

St. Julie Billiart—that a child have strong faith

St. Margaret—that a child may make a good confession and penance

St. Nicholas—that a child may show generosity

St. Agnes—that a child may learn conviction

St. John Bosco—that a child may learn discipline

Day One

St. Monica, you prayed for your son, St. Augustine, to turn his life to Christ, and your prayers were answered. Guide my child to follow God's will. Intercede as a most understanding mother and obtain from God this favor that I desire for my child (mention your request here).

Pray 3 Our Fathers, 3 Hail Marys, 3 Glory Bes

Day Two

Good St. Anne, mother of the most Blessed Virgin Mary, God chose you to give birth to the most perfect of all mothers. Watch over my little saints and angels. Intercede as a most spiritual mother and obtain from God this favor I desire for my child (mention your request here).

Pray 3 Our Fathers, 3 Hail Marys, 3 Glory Bes

Day Three

Blessed Virgin Mary, sweet mother of the Child Jesus, your unquestioning yes to God's will that you be a mother, our Blessed Mother, will live in the hearts of all people forever. Teach my child to seek God's will and to answer yes. Intercede as a most loving mother and obtain from God this favor that I desire for my child (mention your request here).

Say 3 Our Fathers, 3 Hail Marys, 3 Glory Bes

Day Four

St. Maria Goretti, patroness of teenage girls, you resisted sin even at the point of death. Teach my child your deep understanding of forgiveness and help her to be an example to others. Intercede as a most obedient child of God and obtain from God this favor that I desire for my child (mention your request here).

Say 3 Our Fathers, 3 Hail Marys, 3 Glory Bes

Day Five

St. Julie Billiart, you instructed young people in the faith during the most unpopular times and circumstances. Help my child to be filled with that faith. Intercede as a most faith-filled servant and obtain from God this favor that I desire for my child (mention your request here).

Say 3 Our Fathers, 3 Hail Marys, 3 Glory Bes

Day Six

St. Margaret of Scotland, you raised seven sons and two daughters and advocated fasting, almsgiving, penance, and confession. Give my child the strength to hold firm to her beliefs. Intercede as a most persistent leader and obtain from God this favor that I desire for my child (mention your request here).

Say 3 Our Fathers, 3 Hail Marys, 3 Glory Bes

Day Seven

St. Nicholas, patron of children, you were always willing to give to those in need. Teach my child to know the needs of others and to care for those needs. Intercede as a most generous giver and obtain from God this favor that I desire for my child (mention your request here).

Say 3 Our Fathers, 3 Hail Marys, 3 Glory Bes

Day Eight

St. Agnes, patroness of girls, you were put to death because you chose to consecrate yourself to Christ. Show my child the path to true conviction so that she may be an example to others. Intercede as a most pure martyr and obtain from God this favor that I desire for my child (mention your request here).

Say 3 Our Fathers, 3 Hail Marys, 3 Glory Bes

Day Nine

St. John Bosco, you are the great example of patience with young people. Teach my child your way of discipline without anger so she may lead others to Christ with love and kindness. Intercede as a most patient disciple and obtain from God this favor that I desire for my child (mention your request here).

Say 3 Our Fathers, 3 Hail Marys, 3 Glory Bes

A Rosary for my Child

Joyful Mysteries
(use for meditation on Mondays & Saturdays)

1. The Annunciation

"Behold, I am the handmaid of the Lord. May it be done to me according to your word."

Luke 1:38

Mary, teach my child to always say yes to God's will. Help him to pray about and accept this call even when he may not fully understand where the Spirit is leading him. May he humbly accept the will of the Father and never be afraid to follow Christ.

1 Our Father, 10 Hail Marys, 1 Glory Be

We adore you, O Christ, and we praise you because by your Holy Cross, you have redeemed the world.

2. The Visitation

"Blessed are you among women and blessed is the fruit of your womb. My soul proclaims the greatness of the Lord; my spirit rejoices in God my savior."

Luke 1:42, 46–47

Mary, that my child could proclaim the greatness of your Son to those he meets. Help my child in his daily meetings with friends and family. Allow him to find simple pleasures and joy with his sibling(s), his parents, his grandparents, and/or his extended family. Teach him to be an example of charity in this world.

1 Our Father, 10 Hail Marys, 1 Glory Be

We adore you, O Christ, and we praise you because by your Holy Cross, you have redeemed the world.

3. The Birth of Jesus

"While they were there, the time came for her to have her child, and she gave birth to her firstborn son. She wrapped him in swaddling clothes and laid him in a manger, because there was no room for them in the inn."

Luke 2:6–7

Mary, you gave birth to your Son in a lowly stable. Help my child to realize that in the simplest things in life, there he will find Christ. Teach him to detach himself from worldly goods and know that warmth and beauty await in the lowliest of places, in the simplest of mangers.

1 Our Father, 10 Hail Marys, 1 Glory Be

We adore you, O Christ, and we praise You because by your Holy Cross, you have redeemed the world.

4. The Presentation of Jesus in the Temple

"When the time came, they brought the child up to Jerusalem to present him to the Lord."

Luke 2:22

Mary, you took Jesus to present Him in the temple out of obedience to the law. Help my child to always obey the laws of the Church, to follow God's commandments. Keep him pure of heart and mind and never let him wander far from your holy face.

1 Our Father, 10 Hail Marys, 1 Glory Be

We adore you, O Christ, and we praise you because by your Holy Cross, you have redeemed the world.

5. The Finding of the Child Jesus in the Temple

"After three days they found Jesus in the temple, sitting among the teachers and asking them questions."

Luke 2:46

Mary, just as you and Joseph sought and found your Son, show my child the way to seek Jesus. When he is lost, hopeless or scared, teach him that he may always find rest in Jesus, comfort in the Church. Help him to be about the business of the Father.

1 Our Father, 10 Hail Marys, 1 Glory Be

We adore you, O Christ, and we praise you because by your Holy Cross, you have redeemed the world.

Sorrowful Mysteries

(use for meditation on Tuesdays & Fridays)

1. The Agony in the Garden

"My Father, if it is possible, let this cup pass from me; yet, not as I will, but as you will."

Matthew 26:39

Mary, teach my child the power of prayer. Give my child the strength to endure all the hardships life has to offer. Help her to always be open to follow the will of God.

1 Our Father, 10 Hail Marys, 1 Glory Be

We adore you, O Christ, and we praise you because by your Holy Cross, you have redeemed the world.

2. The Scourging of Jesus at the Pillar

"But He was pierced for our offenses, crushed for our sins. Upon Him was the chastisement that makes us whole, by His stripes we were healed."

Isaiah 53:5

Mary, your Son was beaten and never swayed from his pure act of love for his children. Help my child to know that Jesus did all of this to free us from our sins, to heal us. Help her to understand and to know the purity of God's love for her.

1 Our Father, 10 Hail Marys, 1 Glory Be

We adore you, O Christ, and we praise you because by your Holy Cross, you have redeemed the world.

3. The Crowning with Thorns

"The soldiers clothed him in a purple cloak and plaiting a crown of thorns they put it on his head."

Mark 15:17

Mary, even though your Son was mocked and spit upon, he never wavered. He always kept his eyes on his goal. Help my child to stay on the right path especially when it is the least popular way. Help her to stay focused on heaven.

1 Our Father, 10 Hail Marys, 1 Glory Be

We adore you, O Christ, and we praise you because by your Holy Cross, you have redeemed the world.

4. Jesus Carries His Cross

"And He went out bearing his own cross to the place of the skull, called Golgotha."

John 19:17

Mary, your Son carried his own cross, though weak and suffering, to save all mankind. Help my child to bear her crosses in life with grace and dignity. Help her to have the patience and the strength it takes to follow Christ, despite any ridicule.

1 Our Father, 10 Hail Marys, 1 Glory Be

We adore you, O Christ, and we praise you because by your Holy Cross, you have redeemed the world.

5. The Crucifixion

"And bowing his head, he gave up his spirit."

John 19:30

Mary, no greater expression of love has ever been shown as your Son's sacrifice of his own life for us. Give my child a heart of love, totally selfless love. Teach her to love unconditionally.

1 Our Father, 10 Hail Marys, 1 Glory Be

We adore you, O Christ, and we praise you because by your Holy Cross, you have redeemed the world.

Glorious Mysteries

(for meditatation on Wednesdays & Sundays)

1. The Resurrection of Jesus

"The angel said: 'Do not be afraid...He is not here, He is risen as He said.'"

Matthew 28:5–6

Mary, when Jesus rose from the dead, he brought new life for those who believe. Teach my child that Jesus is alive and always here for him. All he has to do is have faith and ask God for all his needs.

1 Our Father, 10 Hail Marys, 1 Glory Be

We adore you, O Christ, and we praise you because by your Holy Cross, you have redeemed the world.

2. The Ascension of Jesus

"As the apostles looked on, Jesus was taken up into heaven out of their sight."

Acts 1:9

Mary, your son ascended into heaven body and soul to prepare a place for us all. Give my child the hope of a life with your son. Teach him and help him to believe that there is a greater good that we work for in this life.

1 Our Father, 10 Hail Marys, 1 Glory Be

We adore you, O Christ, and we praise you because by your Holy Cross, you have redeemed the world.

3. The Descent of the Holy Spirit

"They were filled with the Holy Spirit and began to speak in tongues as they were given power to speak."

Acts 2:2

Mary, your son gave us the gift of the Holy Spirit to guide us in this life so we may one day be with him again. Help my child to always be open to His Spirit. Teach him the way to follow, to hear, to make a place in his heart for the Spirit to dwell.

1 Our Father, 10 Hail Marys, 1 Glory Be

We adore you, O Christ, and we praise you because by your Holy Cross, you have redeemed the world.

4. The Assumption of Mary in Heaven

"Arise, make haste, my love, my dove, my beautiful one, and come."

Canticles 2:10

Mary, in your Assumption, God gave you the gift of eternal happiness. From your seat in heaven, intercede for my child in his need and have mercy on him. Hold him in your mantle and protect him from all evil.

1 Our Father, 10 Hail Marys, 1 Glory Be

We adore you, O Christ, and we praise you because by your Holy Cross, you have redeemed the world.

5. The Crowning of Mary

"A great sign appeared in the heavens, a woman clothed with the sun, the moon under her feet, and on her head a crown of twelve stars."

Revelation 12:1

Mary, Holy Queen, you are our life and our hope in this world of tears. Watch over my child as his mother. Protect him and help him to love you more each day. Teach him to trust you and to call upon you.

1 Our Father, 10 Hail Marys, 1 Glory Be

We adore you, O Christ, and we praise you because by your Holy Cross, you have redeemed the world.

Luminous Mysteries

(for meditatation on Thursdays)

1. The Baptism of Our Lord

"Later Jesus, coming from Galilee, appeared before John at the Jordan to be baptized by him. John tried to refuse him with the protest, 'I should be baptized by You, yet You come to me!' Jesus answered: 'Give in for now. We must do this if we would fulfill all of God's demands.' So John gave in."

Matthew 3:13–15

Mary, teach my child to follow the laws of the Church. Give her the wisdom and the strength to be open to the plans God has for her. May she always be open to the descent of the Holy Spirit.

1 Our Father, 10 Hail Marys, 1 Glory Be

We adore you, O Christ, and we praise you because by your Holy Cross, you have redeemed the world.

2. The Wedding at Cana

"At a certain point the wine ran out, and Jesus' mother told him, 'They have no more wine.' Jesus replied, ' Woman, how does this concern of yours involve me? My hour has not yet come.' His mother instructed those waiting on the table, 'Do whatever he tells you.'"

John 2:3–5

Mary, your Son followed your request even when it was not part of His plan. May my child follow the requests you have revealed through your appearances. Teach her to pray the rosary, to fast, and to repent. Love her as your daughter and show her the way.

1 Our Father, 10 Hail Marys, 1 Glory Be

We adore you, O Christ, and we praise you because by your Holy Cross, you have redeemed the world.

3. The Proclamation of the Kingdom of God

"After John's arrest, Jesus appeared in Galilee proclaiming the good news of God. 'This is the time of fulfillment. The reign of God is at hand! Reform your lives and believe in the gospel!'"

Mark 1:14–15

Mary, teach my child to believe in the good news your son brought to all. Give her the wisdom to know that there are greater joys waiting for her. Show her the way to continue Jesus' ministry and bring others to His kingdom.

1 Our Father, 10 Hail Marys, 1 Glory Be

We adore you, O Christ, and we praise you because by your Holy Cross, you have redeemed the world.

4. The Transfiguration of Our Lord

"He was transfigured before their eyes. His face became as dazzling as the sun, his clothes as radiant as light. Out of the cloud came a voice which said, 'This is my beloved Son on whom my favor rests. Listen to him.'"

Matthew 17:2, 5

Mary, God revealed to the disciples that Jesus is his beloved son. Teach my child about his radiant glory. Help my child to follow the law and the prophets of old so that someday she may come to know the glory of God in His kingdom.

1 Our Father, 10 Hail Marys, 1 Glory Be

We adore you, O Christ, and we praise you because by your Holy Cross, you have redeemed the world.

5. The Last Supper

"During the meal Jesus took bread, blessed it, broke it, and gave it to his disciples. 'Take this and eat it,' he said, 'this is my body.' Then he took a cup, gave thanks, and gave it to them. 'All of you must drink from it,' he said, 'for this is my blood, the blood of the covenant, to be poured out in behalf of many for the forgiveness of sins.'"

Matthew 26:26–28

Mary, teach my child to know your Son in the breaking of the bread. Give her the passion to share in his meal as often as possible. May she receive the grace she needs to someday share in his heavenly banquet.

1 Our Father, 10 Hail Marys, 1 Glory Be

We adore you, O Christ, and we praise you because by your Holy Cross, you have redeemed the world.

Stations of the Cross for My Child

FIRST STATION

Jesus Is Condemned to Death

Matthew 27:26, Mark 15:15, Luke 23:23–25, John 19:16

Lord, be with my child when he is mocked or made fun of. Children can be so cruel at times. Help my child when others falsely accuse him in his life. Teach him to accept wrongful accusations gracefully and to always be kind to others.

SECOND STATION

Jesus Is Made to Carry His Cross

John 19:17

Lord, help my child to accept any crosses he may be asked to bear in his life. Help him to know that these problems are temporary and with you, he can handle any challenges. Teach him not to complain and to keep in his mind and in his heart the cross you carried for all of us.

THIRD STATION

Jesus Falls the First Time

Matthew 27:31

Lord give my child perseverance to complete the tasks given to him in life. Even though he may stumble or even feel like he's failed, help him to continue to the end. As he learns never to give up, teach him that you will never give up on him. Help him to know that you will always be there to pick him up and help him to finish.

FOURTH STATION

Jesus Meets His Blessed Mother

John 19:25–27

Lord, just as your Mother could not carry your burden, so I cannot do everything for my child. Help him to know that I love him especially when life is at its toughest. If I do everything for him, he will never grow mentally and spiritually. Help me to support him in all he does but also let him be his own person.

FIFTH STATION

Simon Helps Jesus Carry His Cross

Matthew 27:32, Mark 15:21, Luke 23:26

Lord, we all have a little Simon in us. We don't want to help another especially if it may cause us to be laughed at or mocked. Help my child to do the unselfish acts in life. Many times he will see someone in need and not really have the time or the desire to stop. Teach him to do more than just stand by and watch.

SIXTH STATION

Veronica Wipes the Face of Jesus

Luke 23:27

Lord, help my child to be like Veronica, to go out of his way to show compassion to someone less popular. Give him the nerve to step out of the crowd and be different. Teach him that by giving to others, he gives to God. Help him always to be a Christian.

SEVENTH STATION

Jesus Falls the Second Time

Luke 23:26

Lord, some days my child may feel like he just cannot go on in your name. The easier way is not always your way. Be with him, Lord, and help him to get up and continue down the right path. Help him to bear the weight of his crosses with strength and dignity, no matter how unpopular he may feel.

EIGHTH STATION

Jesus Speaks to the Women of Jerusalem

Luke 23:28–31

Lord, help my child to be aware of others around him and their needs. It will be easy to get wrapped up in himself and forget that others have problems, maybe even more serious than his own. Help him to always put others first. Help him to overlook their faults while truly caring for their needs.

NINTH STATION

Jesus Falls for the Third Time

John 19:17

$\mathcal{L}$ord, with your third and final fall, you remind us that no matter how often we fail, you will be there. Teach my child that no matter what he does, no matter how bad he's been, you are always there. He can turn to you, lean on you, trust in you. Your love is unconditional and everlasting.

TENTH STATION

Jesus Is Stripped of His Garments

Luke 23:34

$\mathcal{L}$ord, you were stripped of your clothes and ridiculed in front of crowds of people. Help my son not to talk about others or strip them of their dignity in any way. Teach him when to keep his mouth closed and not to reopen the old wounds of another. Show him your mercy and your kindness.

86

ELEVENTH STATION

Jesus Is Nailed to the Cross

Matthew 27:33–38, Mark 15:22–27, Luke 23:33–34, John 19:18

Lord, help my child to show compassion for those hurt because of their differences. Teach him that nails can be driven into others in many different ways. Laughter and unkind words can often hurt. Teach him to show love and kindness to all people.

TWELFTH STATION

Jesus Dies on the Cross

Matthew 27:46–50, Mark 15:34–37, Luke 23:46, John 19: 28–30

Lord, help my child to understand what it means to sacrifice for another. Help him to accept that life is not all about him. Teach him that it is only in dying to self that he can be brought to eternal life with you. Show him your way.

THIRTEENTH STATION

Jesus Is Taken Down From the Cross

Matthew 27:57–58, Mark 15:42–45, Luke 28:50–52, John 19:38

Lord, you were taken off the cross and placed in your Mothers' arms. Help my child to know that I am always here for him. My arms and my heart are always open to his needs. No matter the hardships or the depths of the difficulties, help me to always be at the foot of the cross for my son.

FOURTEENTH STATION

Jesus Is Placed in the Tomb

Matthew 27:59–61, Mark 15:46–47, Luke 23:53–56, John 19:39–42

Lord, there could be no tougher life than the one lived by your Son. Teach my son that if he remains close to you, his life can also be better in the end. Help him to follow your example to lead a life of goodness and mission, and to bring others closer to you.

The Resurrection

Matthew 28, Mark 16, Luke 24, John 20

Lord, it is in your rising that we are brought to new life in Christ. Help my son to rise above his own failures and his own sinfulness and live a life of love for God. Show him the way to a better life, the road that leads back to You. Help him always to rise to the occasions brought on by this life so that in his death, he will rise to be with you forever.

For Other Children

Blessed Teresa of Calcutta,
    you showed us how to love the poor, the homeless,
    the sick.
You were the perfect example of love for all God's
    people, especially His children.
Teach us to open our hearts to those in need,
    those children who have no parents or whose
    parents do not care for them.
Help us to be aware of every child so that we may hear
    them calling in their silence,
    in their hurting, in their hunger.
Help my child see all others as her sisters and brothers.
Show us the way to be Christ to others, to all God's
    children.

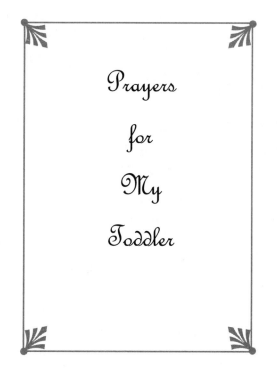

Prayers

for

My

Toddler

First Steps

Dear Lord, my baby took his first steps today.
His first steps toward independence.
As I watch him teetering from side to side,
    I worry about his years ahead.
Help me to keep him on the right track.
Walk with his every step
    so he will not falter in life.
As his baby steps build, keep him in your care.
Bumps and bruises may be part of life, but
I pray they remain a minor part of his life.
May he always stay safe in the palm of your hand.
Amen.

Daycare

Dear Angels of God, guardians of my child, watch
over him at daycare.
Watch over his teachers and
let him feel loved by them as if I were there.
Help him to play well with his little friends.
Rid me of any guilty feelings and
help me to remember that the time we spend apart
makes our times together that much more precious.
Sweet heavenly wings, surround my child and keep
him safe.
Amen.

Bedtime

Lord, what a blessing to kneel down with my child
    before he goes to bed and
    teach him to thank you for his day.
He asks you to bless his friends and his family.
May his simple, sincere requests be heard and
    may he always feel comfort in his prayers to you.
May his night prayers remain as sincere as they are
    today and become as routine as brushing his teeth.
Send his angels to watch over him as he sleeps and
    clear his mind that he may receive
    the rest he needs for a bright new tomorrow.
Amen.

Babysitter

Angels, surround my child and his babysitter and
    keep them safe while I'm away.
Protect them from any uncertainties.
Help my child to act as he should and to feel secure.
May his babysitter treat him with patience and
    kindness and
        enjoy her time with him.
Guard them from any possible harm and
    keep them in your embrace.
And may my child be happy upon my return.
Amen.

Discipline

Mary, help my son to learn from this punishment.
May he understand that his discipline at home is to
    teach him life's lessons.
He has to learn that improper action has consequence.
He has to be taught at home before he gets out in
    society and
    learns much more difficult lessons.
Disciplining him is hard for me.
Let him feel my intense love for him,
    especially during these times.
Mary, keep him safely wrapped in your mantle.
Amen.

Potty Training

Lord, bestow patience.
My child has proclaimed readiness
     for another step toward independence.
He's proud of being a big boy and yet
     he gets so frustrated with learning and accidents.
Help him to stay calm and work patiently toward this
     new goal.
Allow me to take the time with him that potty training
     needs.
Give him perseverance and acceptance.
Watch over my little one as he grows and changes.
Amen.

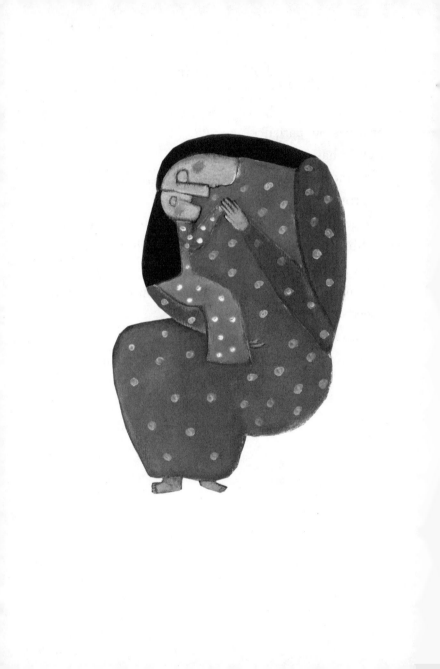

For

My Child's

Early

Years

Play

Dear Lord, my child is going to a friend's house to
   play.
Help him to be a little gentleman,
to be polite to his friend and to the parent or the
   caregiver.
May he share all that he has and understand if he is
   not shared with in return.
Teach him to give, even as a child, without any
   expectations.
Keep him safe from harm and let him have a good
   experience.
Lord, watch over my little man until he returns home.
Amen.

Each Day

Dear Lord,
I pray that as I send my child out into this world
    each and every day,
I have filled his heart and his mind
    with the love of Jesus and of his family.
Often, I'm so filled with the desire to nourish his body
    that I question whether I've nourished his heart.
Give him a heart filled with your love,
    that he may love others as you have loved us.
Lord, stay always beside him while we are apart.
Amen.

First Day of School

Dear Guardian Angel, it's my child's first day of school.

Please be with him today and every day.

He's crying and holding on to me.

Help me to be strong enough to help him let go.

Help me reassure him that he'll be fine.

[As I walk away and then turn back for a peek I see he's in his desk crying. Now the tears are coming to my eyes. Some of the boys he's met before are talking to him and he seems to be settling down.]

Lord, help me to walk away, knowing you will guide him and

guard him until we are together again.

Help him to get along with his classmates and his teacher.

Teach him to open his mind and his heart to school.

Be with him as he learns and as he plays.

Please Guardian Angel, help each school day morning become easier for both of us.

Amen.

School Morning

Lord, as I wake my child for school
    may I help prepare him to face a new day of
    exciting possibilities.
May he be grateful for the chance to learn and
    open to the teaching he receives.
Help him to love his school,
    to embrace the challenges set before him,
    to enjoy his teachers and his classmates.
Keep them all in your care and
    bring us back together safely at the end of this day.
Amen.

Learning to Read

Lord, my child is learning to read.

What complete joy is on his face as he works through
the words on the pages of books I have read to him
before.

It has happened so suddenly.

He's learning many things at one time and quickly
becoming independent.

I tell him daily how proud I am of him.

Reading opens the door to a world of new adventures
and excitement.

Lord, keep his choices moral.

May he understand and learn from his reading and
may he love reading all his life.

This is a wonderful time for him and
I thank you, Lord, for giving us the time to spend
together reading.

Amen.

Money

Lord, we all know that money is the root of all evil.
Every child wants more "things."
Teach my child what is truly important in life.
Show her that all the material possessions in this world
cannot make her happy.
You can give her happiness.
May her spiritual desires always outweigh her material
desires.
Help my child to know that true riches are from
heaven.
More precious than pearls are your gifts.
To gain the riches of this world and to lose heaven—
help my child avoid this tragedy.
Amen.

Prayers

for

My Child's

Middle

Years

Playing Sports

St. Sebastian, watch over my child during his game
   today.
Pray for him and ask God to
      help him to play hard and to do his best,
      and to have fun.
Teach him to be kind and fair to his opponent.
Guide his coach to make good decisions
      and his entire team to have good sportsmanship.
As in his athletics, may my child strive diligently
      and tirelessly
      to win the game of life and score the final goal
      of heaven.
Amen.

Taking Tests

St. Thomas Aquinas,

you led those of your time with open generosity.
Guide my child to do well on her test.
She is prepared but anxious.
Please pray for her.
Ask God to calm her fears,
enlighten her mind and

give her the wisdom and the knowledge

she needs to perform her best.
Amen.

Loss of a Pet

St. Francis, comfort my child during this time. She
    loved (mention pet's name) and
is having a difficult time understanding his death.
    Fill her with your peace
and calm her anxiety.
I know time will heal her of this pain,
    but for now, please comfort her little heart.
Your kindness to all living creatures
    is a beautiful example to us all.
Teach my child to live a simple life and
    to continue to love all living creatures.
Show her compassion during her sadness
    and help her to move on.
Amen.

Online

Computers can open so many doors for our children, Lord.

Help them to use computers wisely and safely.

Guide my child that he may not use instant messaging to slander others.

Watch over his choice of sites especially away from home where there is less supervision.

May he be a witness for the good uses of technology.

Guide his choices today and always.

Amen.

Television

St. Clare, watch over my child's choice of television
shows, especially when I am not around.
Television can be such a great tool
for learning useful information but
it can also fill her mind with harmful suggestions.
Guide her decisions even if they are not popular with
her friends.
Teach her to walk away from the filth and not be afraid
to stand up for her beliefs.
St. Clare, help my child to be able to "look into that
mirror daily" and see a face filled with the love of
Christ.
Amen.

Note: St. Clare is named the patroness of television
because of her ability to see far-off places and events.

Transition

Lord, change is always difficult.

Help my child in making new friends and
    meeting new people.

One minute she seems excited and the next minute
    she's nervous.

Calm her fears and anxieties.

Allow her to be open to the gift of
    fresh, new opportunities.

Give her a welcoming heart so that this transition may
    be smooth and joyful.

As always, watch over her daily Lord, especially when
    we are apart.

Amen.

For

My

Adolescent

Child

115

Full Potential

St. Cecilia, guide my child
to reach her full potential in all her works.
Teach her to use the talents that God has given her
to make a difference in this world.
As you sang to the Lord in your heart,
guide my child to be pure in mind and heart,
and to always pursue the will of God.
Amen.

Commitment

"He summoned the crowd with his disciples and said to them, 'Whoever wishes to come after me must deny himself, take up his cross, and follow me.'"

Mark 8:34

Lord, help my child
> to set aside the pleasures of the world
> and commit herself to you and to your words.

Help her to know that through total commitment to
> the cross she will win everlasting life.

She has played sports and been a part of other
> organized groups.

She knows what it is to commit her time and her
> talents to one thing.

Help her "one thing" to be heaven.

Show her that by following your commandments,
> by attending Mass, by practicing her faith, she will
> win the game.

Help me to be a good example of commitment to you.

Teach both of us your ways, so we may be with you in
> the end.

Amen.

Friendship

"A faithful friend is a sturdy shelter; he who finds one finds a treasure. A faithful friend is beyond price, no sum can balance his worth. A faithful friend is a life-saving remedy, such as he who fears God finds; for he who fears God behaves accordingly, and his friend will be like himself."

Sirach 6:14–17

Lord, what more is there to say?
Help my child with her choices.
Show her the way to faithful friends.
She tries to go with the popular crowd,
    and for a while all is well.
However, she can be left behind at a moment's notice.
Teach her that in the end,
    sometimes choosing the less popular group
    and always choosing the faith-filled path
    keeps her from being "left behind."
Lord, I stress over her lack of friends and her choice
    of friendships.
Be with her.
Guide her.
Bless her.
May You be her closest friend.
Amen.

Courage

Lord, help my child to know that
    with you even the most impossible situations are
    possible.
His Goliath may be something as simple as a bully at
    school or
    as difficult as an addiction.
It may be pressure from peers that challenge his faith
    or challenge him to choose between right and
    wrong.
Big or small, with you by his side, like David, he can
    defeat any enemy.
Whatever or whoever his Goliaths will be,
    lead him to your side for help.
God, give him the wisdom and the trust to
    conquer his challenges in this life
    so that he may see your face in the next.
Amen.

Balance

St. Claude de la Colombiere, guide my child
    to find balance in his life.
Social events, dating, school work, sporting events,
    clubs—
    sometimes it seems he wants to do it all.
Help him to prioritize.
I know you have a gift of leading souls to Christ.
Keep my child on the right track,
    to stay focused and safe
    spiritually, mentally, and physically.
Amen.

Note: St. Claude de la Colombiere is regarded for his devotion to the Heart of Christ, which provided a source of balance and spiritual strengthening.

Call

"Immediately they left their boat and their father and followed him."

Matthew 4:22

Lord, help my child
be strong enough in her faith
to leave all her material possessions, all her earthly desires, and follow you.
When she is tempted to turn away from you
because there is something "more fun," a camp out, a sporting event,
help her to choose you.
Your path may not always be the popular path
or the easy path
but it is the right path.
Help her to answer yes to your call.
Amen.

Peer Pressure

Lord, the choices in this world that our children have to make are rough.

There are so many opportunities for the abuse of drugs and alcohol and sex.

I cannot protect my child from every situation.

She will have tough choices.

Peer pressure is difficult for all of us.

Lord, stay close to my child.

Help her to make decisions that will keep her safe.

If she is made fun of because of her convictions, help her walk away.

Shield her from embarrassment.

She knows what is right.

May she be an example of good fun, that others may change their ways.

Keep her in your care and bring her safely home.

Amen.

Pro-Life

St. Gianna Beretta Molla, you followed the Blessed
Virgin Mary's example of
loving one's "own in the world and loving them to
the end."
Bless my child with this selfless love for human life.
Teach her how fragile and how precious is another's
life.
May she never take the gift of life for granted.
Give her the strength to stand firm for humans' right
to life.
St. Gianna, help my child to follow your example of
witnessing to the true love of Christ and to
human life.
Amen.

Note: Saint Gianna Molla was a devout Catholic and a
skilled doctor. In 1962, pregnant with her fourth child,
she was advised to abort the child because of an ovarian
cyst that made the pregnancy risky for Gianna. She
chose to sacrifice her own life for that of her child,
tragically dying a week after the child was born.

For

My

Older

Teen

High School

$\mathcal{D}$ear Lord, my child is changing.
She has less need for me.
I can feel her pulling away and yet
    I want her to always be my little girl.
Guide her during her high school years
    to choose friends who will strengthen her faith
    in you.
Help her to turn to you during her decision making
    when it is obviously not easy for her to come
    to me.
Hold her in your hands Lord,
    that she may feel your presence in these many
    difficult years.
Help me to allow her to grow and yet keep her always
    in my reach.
Space does not necessarily mean distance.
Keep her close, Lord.
Guide her daily.
Amen.

First Job Interview

Holy Spirit, enlighten my child as she goes for her
first job interview.

She's nervous and excited.

Guide her choice of words.

Allow her to discern if the job is truly right for her.

Help her to listen to all that is said and to take time to
make a good, mature decision.

Lead her in wisdom and in truth, today and every day,
to make good, faith-filled decisions.

Bless her interviewer and may they together work
toward what is good for all.

Amen.

Dating

———————————————————

Mary, as these two leave for this big night,
   surround them with your mantle
   that they may act like a lady and a gentleman.
Help these children to have a great night and yet
   to stay within the bounds of responsible fun.
There are too many temptations in this world
   which can cause them to make decisions
   they will regret tomorrow.
Help them to know the importance of moderation.
Pray for them, Mary, and ask your son to return them
   home safely.
Amen.

Driving

St. Nicholas, patron of travelers,
   protect my child every time she is behind the wheel
   of a car or
   with her friends in a car.
Help her to reach her destination safely and
   return home to her family.
Comfort those who have lost loved ones in their
   travels and
   guide us all in our ultimate journey toward the
   kingdom of heaven.
Amen.

Graduation

Lord, my child is graduating from high school.
Most of her friends are going off to different colleges.
Watch over them all as they separate from their
    parents, and from each other.
With hope and prayer I send my child out into this
    world, that she may take with her the values
    and the faith she's been taught.
Lord, be there in her decision making.
Be there in her rising and stay with her each day,
    all day.
I have to let her go and it scares me, Lord.
Give me the strength and wisdom to know that you
    are with her.
Help her to make new friends easily and to do well in
    her classes.
Transitions are tough.
Show her the way to rise above worldly temptations
    and to make good choices.
Lord, send all the saints of heaven to surround and
    protect these children
    and may each of their angels guide them.
Amen.

Choosing a College

Holy Spirit, guide my child to choose a college
that prepares him well for his life's work.
He is capable of doing well in any school but
I want him to be happy, have responsible fun, and
do well.
He tends to follow his friends.
Show him the way to discern his call.
Lead him to make the right decision for himself.
Give him the wisdom to make good choices
so he will stay close to you through his faith and
benefit from good experiences.
Amen.

Leaving Home

Oh Lord, the mixed emotions I have about my child
     leaving home!
I've waited for this day for her to spread her wings,
     and yet, I've dreaded her going out
     into the world alone.
Help her to walk in the light of faith.
Keep her close to you and
     remind her to rely on you for everything.
Help me to let go gracefully; to let her grow.
Now, all those family values that we've taught her
     need to kick in.
May she stay open to your love, your mercy, and your
     guidance.
Lord, bless my child.
Amen.

Loss of Faith

St. Monica, teach me to pray my child back into
    the faith as you prayed for your son, Augustine.
Teach me perseverance and patience.
Intercede for all mothers and
    show us the way to lead our children back to God.
Intercede for our children as you did for your son that
    God might gently guide them
    to know the mercy and goodness of Christ.
My child has gone astray.
Help me to pray him back towards the Lord.
Amen.

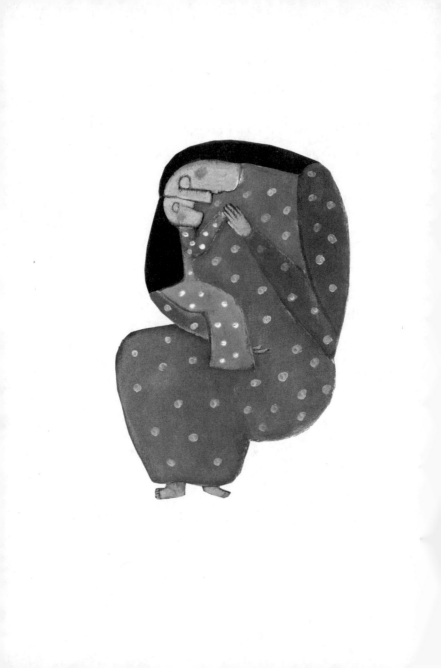

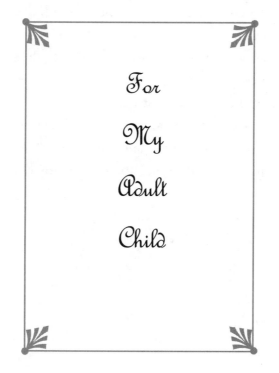

For

My

Adult

Child

Adult Child

St. Maximilian, pray for my son
  so that he will turn to Mary, as you did,
  in times of great pain and frustration.
I know that you, who gave your life for another,
  can certainly turn my son
  in the right direction for help.
Give him the courage to ask God for all he needs,
  and to trust God to guide his way.
St. Maximilian, instill in my son your intense love and
  faith in Jesus.
Amen.

Vocations

Come, Holy Spirit,
    guide my child to know
    the will of God for his life and
    give him the grace to follow his calling.
You have filled him with talents
    far beyond what the world could teach.
Whatever his work, as a religious, an engineer,
    a doctor, a lawyer, a teacher, or something else,
    teach him that by serving others well,
    he serves the Lord.
Show him how to be an example of Christ's love to all
    his co-workers.
Holy Spirit, may your light show through all of us and
    guide us in our work
    so that the love of Christ
    shines for all the world.
Amen.

Example of God's Love

St. Katharine Drexel, you gave your life's fortunes
to care for and serve the poor and the oppressed.
No matter what my child chooses as her life's work,
teach her to be rich in her love for Christ and for
others.
Teach her to share the wealth of her love with those
she meets in life,
especially those who experience poverty
and oppression of the heart.
Help her to be an example of God's undivided love.
Amen.

Single Life

Lord, I pray my child is fulfilled in the single life she
  has chosen.
She is so confident and empowered with such
  incredible goals for her life.
Help her to stay close to you:
    focused on spreading your word,
    focused on being an example of your love.
May her life be complete.
Keep her always in your care.
Amen.

A New Mother

Mary, chosen Mother of the child Jesus,
 bless my daughter as she becomes a mother for the
 first time.
Teach her the importance of spending quality time
 with her child.
Give her the grace to pass the faith to her child and
 to be an example of always doing God's will.
Help her to be a woman with strong conviction.
Give her the strength and the wisdom to turn to you
 and your Son in her need.
Amen.

A New Father

Good St. Joseph, patron of families,
   bless my son as he becomes a father for the first
   time.
Help him to provide well for his family.
Teach him the importance of being a part of his
   child's life, of physically being there for his child.
Make him a loving, tender, caring man
   and fill him with the grace to pass the faith
   on to his child.
This world needs good men with strong convictions
   as examples for our children.
Teach him to use his skills to build a family of God.
Amen.

Praying for Her Child

Lord, may my daughter know the power of praying
for her child.

May she understand the importance of
praying so that this child will return to you
someday.

May she feel your presence that
she will constantly and comfortably ask for
your help.

May she know to call upon the saints and the angels
to protect and guide her child.

Lord, fill my daughter with the desire to
call upon you.

Teach her how to pray for her child.

If I could hand down only one gift
to my child, it would be the power of praying her
child through life.

Amen.

For

My Child's

Most

Serious

Needs

145

Imperfections

Dear Lord,
>   look with compassion on my child
>   as he deals with life in his small world.
Other children can be so cruel.
I know his differences are hard for other children to
>   understand and
>   he's not as quick to learn.
>   Please help him find friends with kind hearts.
Help him to excel in the things he can do and
>   give him the patience and the understanding
>   to deal with others who make fun of his
>   imperfections.
I know he is perfect in your eyes.
Give him a loving heart and a strong will
>   to overcome life's torments.
Amen.

Eating Disorder

St. Padre Pio, please intercede and
   ask God to heal my child of this terrible disease.
She is literally killing herself.
I know she is getting professional help.
Help her to feel my love and my support
   since she won't allow me to be with her.
This is one of those many times where I
   have no control.
I know that the best thing I can do as a mother
   is to pray.
St. Padre Pio, pray your healing words for my daughter
   so God will relieve her sickness.
Amen.

Cancer

St. Peregrine, be with my child as
     she has just been diagnosed with this terrible
     disease.
I cannot handle her suffering,
     and yet she needs me to be strong.
I ask more than ten times a day—Why her Lord?
I'm asking you to intercede
     and ask God, a merciful God, to heal my child.
If there is some greater plan, some reason,
     ask God to heal my heart so that I may
     understand.
Please cradle my child through her suffering and ease
     her pain.
Amen.

Operation

Lord, our baby cries out in constant pain through
countless nights of waking her, swinging her and
sitting up with her.
Now, as I walk her all the way down to the operating
room in her tiny little hospital gown,
I put her in your hands, Lord.
Keep my baby safe and make her well.
Waiting is the hardest but I know you are here with us.
Help this procedure to be successful, Lord.
Bring this child some sweet relief.
Amen.

For the Doctors and Nurses

Sts. Cosmas and Damien, please guide the doctors'
skilled hands as they perform this medical
procedure.
Guide the nurses in their ministry of healing care.
Bless them as the ministers of your healing power, and
help them to heal my child.
Amen.

Hopelessness

St. Jude, sharing the name of the traitor Judas
  has caused you to be the last saint we call upon;
  our last desperate plea.
Intercede for us and
  ask Jesus to be with my child in this most hopeless
  time.
Help her to stay close to Christ, especially during this
  struggle
  when she feels so all alone.
Help her to always feel the saving power of Christ
  and lead her in his mercy.
Amen.

Death of a Friend

Lord, my child's good friend has died
and she is having a difficult time understanding
your will.
She sees the immense sorrow of the parents and her
other friends.
She hears the crying and the questioning.
She longs to see her friend one more time and
yet she knows those times are gone.
She believes in you, Lord, but she's struggling to make
sense of it all.
Help her, Lord. In your infinite mercy, console her.
Give her the gifts of time and understanding.
Embrace her helplessness and comfort her in your
arms.
Amen.

Unable to Have Children

Lord, You know our every need.
You know how badly my daughter wants to have
   children
   and has been unable to conceive.
We do not know the plans you have for us
   but help us to be willing to accept all you give and
   all you withhold.
If it is your will, bless my daughter and her husband
   with a healthy baby.
Otherwise, in your great mercy, help them to
   understand your will and
   to stay close to you.
Show them your compassion and
   give them the strength to persevere in your name.
Amen.

Miscarriage

$\mathcal{L}$ord, she's heard it all:
"There was something wrong."
"In God's time."
"You can have another."
"God's will."
"It was God's plan."
"God's mercy."
Lord, where are you in all of this?
She's really having a hard time understanding.
Stay with her during this faith struggle.
As her baby goes back to you, teach her to accept this
    sacrifice, this challenge.
Give her strength and trust and faith.
Amen.

Struggling Marriage

St. Angela Merici, my daughter is struggling with her
marriage.

Pray that she stays close to God during all of this and
that she makes unselfish decisions.

The world makes it so simple to stray
from what is right and just.

In your goodness, help my daughter in her time of
frustration.

Help her in her reconciliations in life to become a
faithful witness to Jesus.

Amen.

Single Parent

$\mathcal{D}$ear Lord, bless my child as she raises her own child
as a single parent.

Give her the strength to be both mother and father,
and the time to enjoy life with her child.

When she looks at the big picture, it can be so
overwhelming.

Help her to take one day at a time, and to stay close to
you and your Mother.

With you, she is never alone.

You gave us one another for support.

Help her as a single parent to feel the support of
others and
help others to come to her side in times of need.

May we all be one family in you.

Amen.

Death of a Child

Dear Lord, I'm lost. I'm angry.
I cannot find you in any of this and yet I know I
    cannot go on without you
I know in my heart of hearts that my child is safe
    within your loving arms now for all eternity.
I know he is free from the pain and sorrow this life has
    to offer.
But, I carried him. I love him and I miss him.
Give me the strength to carry on here on earth until I
    too can be reunited with you.
If it is your will Lord, mend this broken heart and
    teach me how to bear the burden of going on
    without my child.
Teach me to graciously accept the help of others.
They have no idea what I'm going through and yet,
    they want to "do something."
I want everyone to leave me alone.
Lord, give me strength and faith
    that my sorrow may be some source of good for
    another.
Allow me to cling to the examples of your Mother.
Show me her ways, O Lord.
Amen.

JULIE CRAGON is the mother of six, ages 3 through 16. She lives in Nashville, Tennessee where she and her husband manage St. Mary's Bookstore. This is her first book.

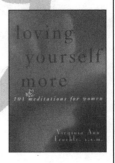